The Little
Visualisation

by
Rachel Walmsley
& Rick Armstrong

The Little Book Of Visualisation

Fisher King Publishing
The Studio, Arthington Lane,
Pool-in-Wharfedale,
LS21 1JZ,
England.

ISBN 978-1-906377-13-7

The Little Book of
Visualisation

Rachel Walmsley is the founder of Succeed Training and Development Ltd and a partner at Mentor – UK. Rachel works as a consultant in business and in schools, using transformational learning tools such as peer coaching and visualisation. She runs 'Creating a Coaching Culture' a course which has been successfully implemented by over 100 schools nationally.

Rick Armstrong is CEO of Mentor-UK, he is an inspirational speaker and trainer who works with companies and organisations around the world in leadership and management development.

The authors believe that the power of words and use of visualisation techniques can dramatically alter perspectives to create positive change for all.

**Rachel Walmsley
& Rick Armstrong**

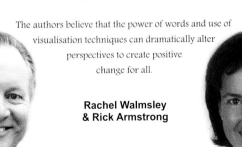

*The authors would like to thank
Richard Gale, Christine Weston
and John Lawrence for their
assistance in editing this book.*

We have included techniques in this little book which we have been using for many years. Each visualisation has helped transform our lives. We use the visualisations ourselves on a regular basis to create even more happiness and fulfilment. None of the information can be truly original as the techniques have evolved over time; however, we have presented it in a format which makes it easy to follow, any time, in any place.

Our interest in writing this book is based on two basic concepts: a belief in the vastness of human potential, and an understanding that the amount of personal fulfilment we can experience is limitless. On average each human being only uses around 10% of their potential. We wonder what the world would be like if we all decided to live life to the full?

Using the visualisations will help you to get the very best out of life. You have a very powerful internal influence over your own thoughts, when you realise this, all things become possible. This book is also designed to help you when you have moments of doubt or stuck-ness. These are the times when it can be hardest to remember that you have power. You always have control over your own thoughts and every positive thought you create makes a difference.

The Little Book of Visualisation is designed to be carried in your pocket. You can read it on the bus, whilst in a queue, sitting on a train, whilst needing a moment of relaxation. It is also designed for use in groups, either in the workplace, or in schools and colleges.

If you are reading the visualisations to others, strive to use a gentle tone of voice to help the listener (s) to feel comfortable and relaxed. As you are reading, ensure that you are also in this feeling state yourself.

As you settle into the desired state, whether it is Wellness, Gratitude or Connection with Nature, many wonderful things will start to happen as a result, and as such you will have a deeper experience of life.

You may want to use the book in a mediation class, counselling or coaching session, as part of a class at school or team meeting, or with a colleague or client.

The most important thing is to enjoy this process and to have fun.

We believe in the magic of life. You are truly amazing. We hope you enjoy using this book.

Visualisation is the ability to use your imagination and your feelings to energise an idea and gradually draw it into your reality. It can be used to build confidence or to enhance wellbeing and to visualise a successful outcome. The technique has been widely used in sport over the last 30 years to improve all aspects of performance.

There is strong evidence that it was used by Tibetan monks in the middle ages but other people say it goes back far further, to the ancient civilisations.

When doing the visualisation exercises it best to find a time when you will not to be disturbed for 10 -15 minutes and to feel in a relaxed state.

You do not need to see vivid pictures. You may get a sense or strong feeling whilst you are visualising. Visualisation takes practice, the more you do it, the more effective it becomes.

Believe it or not, you are already using visualisation every day without realizing it, as every thought and feeling is creating your life. If you become aware of negative thoughts or beliefs it is best not to fight with them. Just accept they are there and realign to your positive images and thoughts.

'Visualisation Toolkit'
Separate to this pocket book we have created a 'Visualisation Toolkit', in which we show you further ways to use visualisation using processes such as:

Goal setting
Strategic visioning

How to teach visualization

As you consciously use this process, you will experience some amazing results.

We encourage you to use this approach in the workplace, with your team, in your personal life, or as a teacher or educator, or as chair of a committee or school council. It can even be used in the boardroom to help you move towards your organisational aims. The pack will help you to find the best approach needed to get the outcomes you would like.

Based on the visualisations in the book, we encourage you to make up your own positive visualisations to suit your own particular goals and intentions. If you take the time to use the visualisations, this book will change your life! *Thank you for using it.*

Contents

Find a way to relax and feel comfortable wherever it is you are lying or sitting. Be aware of any tensions you feel. As you mentally scan your body, bring awareness to each part of it and tell yourself that it is now OK to relax.

Take a few deep breaths and as you breathe out just imagine letting go of all the tension and stress in your body. Tell yourself, it's great to relax, it's OK to feel good.

Bring your attention to your head and notice what is happening within – how does it feel? Allow your head to totally relax. Bring your attention to your face, notice what is happening in your face; maybe you could even smile, see what that's like. Feel all the muscles relaxing.

If there is any tension in your jaw, just let it go. Then just focus on your breathing. Each time you take a breath, imagine yourself becoming more deeply relaxed. Now move down your body into your neck and shoulders. If there is any tension in your shoulders, just let it go and allow yourself to sink more deeply into the floor or chair.

Move down into your hands and your arms. It's OK for them to relax, imagine all the tension draining away. Remember all the things your hands do, and the service they provide for you, it is good for them to relax too.

Focus on your chest and your stomach. Now your lower back, and your buttocks. So much tension can be held in these areas, without you realising. Let them relax too.

Each time you breathe out, feel all stresses and strains being released from your body. Allow yourself to relax even more deeply. Focusing on your thighs, relax them too, and your knees, calves, and your feet. Remember all the service that your feet provide for you. Bring your attention to your toes and any tension in your toes, just let it go.

Now as you breathe in, imagine inhaling white light that fills up your whole body, it fills you with peace and contentment. White light pours in through your nostrils and reaches every part of your body. Feel every part of your body vibrant and peaceful. Do this two or three times.

Now you will be feeling more calm, more peaceful and at home in yourself.

Allow yourself to relax and feel completely at ease. If there is any tension in your body, allow it to dissolve. Take a few deep breaths. Each time you breathe in, count slowly from 10 to 1 and feel more relaxed at each count.

Imagine yourself sitting in a peaceful and relaxing place in nature on a warm summers day. It could be near a tree, in a clearing, on a hilltop, or in a field.

Feel the warmth of the sun filling your entire body, soak up this sunshine, and allow it to drench your body, you are feeling happy and at peace.

Now see yourself walking on the grass, feel the firmness of

the ground, feel the cool grass beneath your feet, the breeze blowing gently on your face.

Feel as though you are at one with the scene around you. Feel the energy, the life force, the clarity of the air, the radiance of the sunshine. Be aware of the in and the out of your breath, allow yourself to breathe deeply. It feels so good to be free and healthy, and connected to nature at this moment in time, on this warm summer's day.

Everything is quiet, you are alone, notice how the light shimmers and sparkles, how the sun settles on the trees. Stop for a moment, look and listen, all you can hear is the gentle breeze as it moves across the landscape.

Feel the freedom, feel the lightness of being. Be aware of the birds gliding above you in the sky, it's great to have time to be able to watch.

Breathe in the energy of this place and know you can come back here whenever you choose.

After a few moments, in your own time, come back to the room.

See yourself in a beautiful place in nature. Take a few slow, deep breaths and each time you exhale let go of the tensions of the day. Allow yourself to relax.

You are going on a journey to meet your inner guide. This is the wise part of you that always knows the right thing to do and the right situation to be in. It's up to you how you see your inner guide, it could be through your imagination or a gut feeling. Your inner guide is there to help you and give you all the information you need, it is the part of you that you know you can trust.

Think of a question that you would like to ask and just

notice what happens. You may feel all kinds of things, but wait and be still and just see what comes back. Perhaps there are things you have felt confused about lately, about which you could benefit from having some advice.

You may feel yourself receiving an answer. Sit with that. Just relax and get a sense of what is being said to you. If it is coming from your inner guide, it should feel good. It will feel right. Notice how that feels. Your inner guide will always give you positive and supportive advice.

Appreciate this guidance and think of another question that you would like to ask. Is there something else that you are not sure about, something that has been bothering you? See what thoughts or feelings come to mind. You may get visual images, words or feelings that come to you but generally it will feel good.

Another name for your inner guide is your intuition. Whenever you need to call on this, you can return here since it is always a part of you. You can come back to this place anytime. All you need to do is ask. Just note how you are feeling now, notice your body. Be aware of yourself. It is now time to come back to the present. Take a few deep breaths and gradually open your eyes.

Gratitude

Find a comfortable position and gradually start to relax. Take a deep breath then exhale slowly. Gradually feel the tension drain out of your body and allow yourself to relax.

Become aware of a time in your life when you felt appreciative of someone or something. Was it a good deed done for you by someone? Who or what in your life do you feel grateful for? Focus on that experience now and allow yourself to feel happy and thankful. Really enjoy this feeling and allow it to get stronger and stronger.

Now imagine all the things in your life for which you are thankful. As you bring each one to mind, intensify the feeling of gratitude, really feel it in your body. Appreciate all the wonderful things as they pass through your mind.

Now focus on something you would like to create in your life. Imagine your desired outcome and feel your success in its achievement. What can you see? What can you feel? What can you hear? Intensify the feelings of it happening right now. Be grateful for already having it.

With this awareness of all the abundance in your life, gradually in your own time come back to the room, to the present moment.

Whenever something wonderful happens in your life, be thankful that your intentions are working, and be pleased for your good fortune.

Allow yourself to relax. Take a few deep breaths and as you breathe out, allow any tensions to drain away through your feet into the floor.

Imagine a time in your life when you were successful. Think of a time when you felt really pleased with an outcome you created and imagine it with intensity. This is an achievement in your life, something you feel really proud of. Allow yourself to experience that feeling of success. What can you see? What can you feel? What can you hear?

You know you have worked hard to achieve this success, you deserve this feeling of achievement. It could be a creative project you have organised, a goal that came to fruition. You feel exhilarated and uplifted. Feel a wave of contentment ride over you. You are a very powerful person with many gifts and talents. All the steps you have taken to bring about this achievement, you can recreate at any time.

As you imagine the experience of success with all its intensity, create an even stronger feeling, double the intensity of the feelings. Breathe in the success, get excited, and feel exhilarated. See yourself doing your best, as your success creates even more of the same.

As you intensify the feelings, now imagine a circle on the floor in front of you. Notice that the circle has a colour. Step inside the circle. Notice what you can hear, smell, and feel. Now step outside the circle and take a few deep breaths. In your own time step back into the circle and triple the intensity of the feelings of success. Now you really feel exhilarated, really celebrate now. This is such a wonderful place to be.

Intensify the colour, allow yourself to be bathed in the light of this beautiful colour. You are filled with radiance. See yourself glowing and full of achievement. Step outside the circle again.

Now, whilst still feeling the glow of this radiance, step back inside the circle and imagine a goal you would like to achieve. Is there something in life that you have wanted to create? Imagine it now. Know that this goal is absolutely within your reach. Each time you breathe in, enjoy the excitement of already having achieved it. Everything that needs to happen to make this a reality is falling into place right now. See the goal as already accomplished. The outcome of this goal is for your highest good and for the highest good of those around you.

Now notice yourself taking the first steps in achieving this. What will you be doing? Make a commitment to do this today.

With a sense of peace at having accomplished your goal, step outside the circle of excellence knowing that whenever you want to experience this success, you can create it. Everything in your life is being created by your intentions.

Life is good to you and you are the creator of your own experience. You create your own experience by intending a positive outcome through your powerful and deliberate intentions. In your own time open your eyes and come back to the room.

Find a comfortable position. Take a few deep breaths and gradually start to relax. As you exhale feel all the tensions draining out of your body.

Imagine yourself getting to grips with a new skill or activity. See yourself as eager and excited about this. You are in a positive and open state to learn. Feel this in as much detail as possible. You have a strong desire to develop your knowledge, and you trust that new information will be absorbed easily and effortlessly.

You are pleased to be in this position, to be able to learn new things. Learning these skills helps you to move forwards in life, towards even more happiness. See yourself being extremely successful in achieving your goals and plans. You are so proud to have mastered your new skill. Visualise yourself receiving your reward or certificate or using your new abilities and perhaps even passing them on to others.

You feel confident and alert. You trust that you will be guided to what you need to know next and that all the most beneficial information will be made available. All your teachers are highly skilled. They are cheering for you and encouraging you toward your goals. You have only positive judgements about yourself. You hear yourself saying: 'I am a brilliant learner,' 'I LOVE learning,' 'I can do it,' 'I can be the best I can be'. This excitement for learning helps you to move forwards very quickly and people around you are amazed at how skilled you have become.

You enjoy being creative as you learn, and you enjoy

trying out new things. You choose the best time of day to study. You are confident and positive about dealing with any new challenges. All the skills and knowledge you have previously acquired stand you in good stead as you move powerfully forwards. You are loving this!!

Relax and find a comfortable position. Let any tensions drain out of your body. Start with your feet and move towards your head and imagine relaxing every muscle in your body. Let the tension flow out into the ground. Breathe slowly and deeply, count gradually from 10 to 1 and feel more relaxed at each count.

You are going to use your imagination to create what you truly want. Think of something that you want to create and picture it clearly, it could be a new car or home, a perfect state of health or improved family relationships. What can you see? Are there any other people around? What is it you'd like to experience? As you see your desired goal in detail, see yourself feeling happy, radiant and filled with energy. You feel joyful.

Now make the decision to only focus on the things that make you happy. What brings you joy? Everything you experience is a reflection of what you believe and you become what you focus on. Choose now to only focus on what makes you happy. Every moment is a new opportunity to create your own life.

See yourself as an artist with a blank canvas, creating a picture of your life as you would like it to be. Start to feel the feelings of already having what you want. See your desired situation in detail. Feel excited about it. Each time you see the picture, feel even more joyful and excited. Think big; see the options that feel most alive to you. Know that you are allowing this situation to happen by focussing clearly on it and knowing that it is possible.

Knowing that you can create what you want by your intentions, commit to only focus on the things that are aligned with what feels good for you. See yourself mixing

with people who are aligned with your highest goals.
You are a powerful creator. Now consider one way that
you will use your own power of focus on your desired
outcome. Gradually in your own time, open your eyes and
come back to the room.

Relax and find a comfortable position. Focus on your breathing and each time you exhale, see any tensions draining out of your body, relax your whole body and enjoy the sensation of being at peace.

How much money would you like to have? Picture the amount in your mind. Now see yourself holding all this money in your hands, see it glowing. You feel happy and fulfilled that you now have everything you have asked for. Be thankful and excited. What can you see? What can you feel? What can you hear?

See yourself using the money for good purposes. What will you use the money for? Know that it is alright to have as much as you need.

Affirm that you always have more money coming in than going out and that money serves your higher purpose.

You have the power to create more and more abundance.

Money flows to you easily and effortlessly. It is easy to make money and it brings you joy. There is no reason to make a big effort to earn money, if flows to you as if by magic.

See yourself living your life's purpose, sharing your gifts and talents with the world and being rewarded highly. Imagine offering your skills to the world and it being of such value that people are willing to pay you highly.

There is plenty of money in the world. All you need to do is be happy to receive it and take action to share your skills with others. All around you are truly amazed at the abundance you have created.

See money coming to you in ways you never expected. See

yourself as financially independent and free, knowing that your prosperity benefits others.

Abundance is your birthright and you are in a stronger position than ever before to create this. The universe supports you in having everything that you ever dreamed possible. Make a commitment today that you will take the next step that is needed towards creating abundance. Think of what the next step will be and commit to it.

And now with all this abundance in mind, gradually in your own time, open your eyes.

Relax and find a comfortable position. Take several deep breaths and allow any tension to drain out of your body. Each time you exhale see the tensions draining out of you and into the ground.

Imagine the type of work that you would love to do. See yourself doing it now. See it in as much detail as possible. How do you feel? Who are you relating to? What are people saying to you? Ensure it is really positive. See yourself having fun, expressing yourself, really using all your skills and talents. Know that it is possible to create this kind of work – that this is within your reach.

See yourself being financially rewarded. You are being paid more money than you expected. Watch the money flow into your hands – feel the crispness of the notes or cheques. Imagine yourself feeling at home in the work and enjoying the company of co-workers or associates. Really enjoy the environment you are in, imagine every detail.

You are fully expressive and creative. This is a positive healthy working environment where you and others all treat each other well. There is honest and open communication. There is integrity in your work. You are so happy to be engaged in something which is so rewarding and you feel proud that you have created this.

You have the power to create fulfilling work for yourself. You may not know how it will happen at this stage. However, you feel confident that you have everything in your power to create the work that you love.

Your work is an expression of the best part of you. You are here to be a positive influence through your work.

Everything you do in relation to your work is moving you further towards your highest fulfilment. Know that all this is possible and is happening much more easily than you expected.

Now gradually in your own time open your eyes and come back to the room.

Creating wellness

Sit quietly for a few moments and gradually allow yourself to relax. Become aware of any tensions in your body. If your mind is busy, imagine your thoughts as passing clouds. They are just thoughts, they are not who you are. Take a few deep breaths and exhale slowly.

This is a healing visualisation for your mind and body. As you allow your body to relax and be at peace, you create more and more wellbeing in your life. Perhaps there is a part of your body that would like to feel better? If it had a voice, what would this part of your body say?

As you allow yourself to tune in and listen, it will gradually tell you what it needs. Perhaps you need time to slow down and take life at a gentler pace. Maybe you need more time to allow yourself to have fun and play.

Make your decision today to do what it takes to enjoy life more. What would the next step be towards this? Imagine yourself doing it now. Know that it is entirely possible to have perfect health. You are here to feel alive and happy, maybe you've just forgotten how to do this. It's good to feel alive!

Each time you look in the mirror tell yourself how amazing you are. Appreciate yourself and be thankful for your uniqueness. Say the words: 'I am in perfect health, I look after my body, I am attractive and healthy'.

Right now, enjoy all the wonderful sensations in your body. You feel attractive and alive. Breathe deeply, and each time you breathe in, see each area of your body filled with white light. See yourself as full of radiant white light. Make the intention that each part of your body is becoming more and more vibrant and healthy. See yourself as full of energy.

Now that your body is radiant and glowing, know that you can create this every day and at any time you may need to.

Take a few more deep breaths and gradually in your own time come back to the room.

Relax and sit or lie comfortably. Take a few deep breaths and exhale slowly. Gradually feel your body become more and more relaxed.

We are going to visualise your success. See yourself preparing for your interview. Notice how you are feeling. Perhaps you are excited or nervous? Also notice that you are feeling well prepared, and you are pleased with yourself that you have completed everything on your checklist and left no stone unturned in your preparations. You are extremely proud of all the hard work you have done so far. Each time you think about your interview, see yourself walking out at the end, having been successful.

Feeling relaxed and confident, imagine you are walking

into the interview room, knowing that whatever comes along, you will handle it confidently. As you go into the room, make eye contact with the interviewer or examiner. You smile and sit down in a composed manner. You exchange a few words and then they ask you the first question. You realise you know the answer. The words roll off your tongue. Then you are asked the second question to which you also know the answer. You feel very pleased with yourself. You enjoy feeling confident and well prepared.

The third question is a bit more tricky and demands more thought. However, even though you are not entirely sure how to answer it, you know that you will find the right thing to say. You never doubt your ability. Once you get through this tricky question, you know you can get through anything that may come along.

All the way through the interview, you carry the belief in

yourself, knowing you've done the preparation, you've done the work. You are passionate about this subject and you want the interviewers to know about it.

At the end of the interview you are extremely happy. You are on a high. You gave your best and you feel a sense of achievement. You always knew this was possible.

See yourself smiling and saying good bye, walking out of the room. Intensify the feeling of achievement and satisfaction, you got the outcome you wanted. You are very pleased.

Gradually in your own time, open your eyes and come back to the room.

Find a comfortable position and take a few deep breaths. Gradually allow yourself to relax. Counting down from 10 to 1, with each breath, you feel even more relaxed.

Now start to think about all the things in life that you enjoy the most. What makes your heart sing? Is it a hobby or interest, or being with people? What kind of activities do you really enjoy? Focus on them now. Really enjoy this.

Remember a time when you were younger? What activities did you enjoy the most? What motivated you? If there was something you found extremely rewarding and would get absorbed by, see yourself doing it now. What can you see? What can you feel? What can you hear?

Now ask yourself: 'What matters most to me in life?' 'If I were to die tomorrow, is there something that I would like to have done?' ' What kind of contribution would I like to have made?' Is there something you feel passionate about? Now see yourself doing this, using all your talents and natural abilities.

Maybe you are here to help others, to make a difference, to help the world in some way. Ask yourself: 'What is my purpose and mission in life?' Feel yourself doing this now and really enjoying it. Whatever brings you the most happiness is often what you are meant to be doing.

Now decide to follow your purpose and to allow it to guide you through life. If you ever doubt what matters to you, you can come back to this. You are pleased about what you have discovered, it makes life easy. You are thankful for the opportunities you now have. Whatever you are doing also benefits others. You know that whatever lays ahead that you will always be guided, and that you have all the resources you need. You are a creative, capable and powerful human being.

Take a few more deep breaths and gradually in your own time come back to the room, knowing that you can recreate this passion for your purpose whenever the need arises.

What is your personal visualisation? Make notes here.

What is your personal visualisation? Make notes here.

What is your personal visualisation? Make notes here.